Britain's Airborne Forces of WWII

Britain's Airborne Forces of WWII

Uniforms and Equipment

Mark Magreehan

FRONTLINE BOOKS

First published in Great Britain in 2020 by
Frontline Books
An imprint of
Pen & Sword Books Ltd
Yorkshire – Philadelphia

Copyright © Mark Magreehan 2020

ISBN 978 1 52677 946 5

A CIP catalogue record for this book is
available from the British Library.

Typeset by Mac Style
Printed and bound in India by Replika Press Pvt. Ltd.

MIX
Paper from
responsible sources
FSC
www.fsc.org
FSC® C016779

Pen & Sword Books Limited incorporates the imprints of Atlas, Archaeology,
Aviation, Discovery, Family History, Fiction, History, Maritime, Military, Military
Classics, Politics, Select, Transport, True Crime, Air World, Frontline Publishing,
Leo Cooper, Remember When, Seaforth Publishing, The Praetorian Press,
Wharncliffe Local History, Wharncliffe Transport, Wharncliffe True Crime
and White Owl.

For a complete list of Pen & Sword titles please contact

PEN & SWORD BOOKS LIMITED
47 Church Street, Barnsley, South Yorkshire, S70 2AS, England
E-mail: enquiries@pen-and-sword.co.uk
Website: www.pen-and-sword.co.uk

Or

PEN AND SWORD BOOKS
1950 Lawrence Rd, Havertown, PA 19083, USA
E-mail: Uspen-and-sword@casematepublishers.com
Website: www.penandswordbooks.com

Contents

Acknowledgements

The writing of the book has been greatly assisted by access to images kindly provided by the Airborne Assault museum at Duxford IWM. I would like to especially thank Jon baker the curator of Airborne Assault museum. Thanks should also go to my partner Sarah for pressing me to do something with all my junk in the garage. Also Robert Hilton for his support through the years. Finally I would like to acknowledge the advice and patience of those at Frontline Books and Pen and Sword books.

Chapter 1

1940: The Formation of British Airborne Forces

The British Commandos were formed in 1940, on the order of the Prime Minister Winston Churchill. In response to defeats in Norway and France, the call came for specially-trained troops that would 'develop a reign of terror down the enemy coast'. Initially they were to be a small force of Army volunteers who were to carry out limited 'hit and run' raids into enemy-occupied territory.

By the autumn of 1940 more than 2,000 men had volunteered for Commando training, and what became known as the Special Service Brigade was formed into twelve units called Commandos.

Early Commando training was done on a unit basis with selected officers and NCOs attending the Special Training Centre at Lochailort in the west of Scotland, then returning to their units to pass on the skills learnt. In February 1942 the Special Training Centre training moved to Achnacarry in the Highlands, which had been used as a holding wing for Lochailort. It was renamed the Commando Depot (later re-designated as the Commando Basic Training Centre) and became the centre for all Commando training.

Initially the volunteers at Achnacarry went through an intensive six-week course. Training concentrated on speed marches, personal fitness, weapons training, map reading, climbing, small boat operations and demolitions both by day and by night, finishing in a confirmatory live-fire beach assault (raid).

Each Commando would number around 450 men commanded by a lieutenant colonel. They were subdivided into troops of seventy-five men and further divided into fifteen-man sections. Commandos were all volunteers seconded from other British Army regiments and retained their own cap badges, with the exception of No. 2 Commando who adopted the fighting knife as their cap badge, and remained on their regimental roll for pay purposes.

Churchill's memo dated 22 June 1940 to his chief military adviser General Ismay was the start of British airborne forces. A parachute school was established at Ringway Airport near Manchester, and No. 2 Commando was chosen as the first training unit for parachute duties. This small nucleus quickly grew and was renamed 11th Special Air Service Battalion and ultimately, on 1 August 1942, The

Parachute Regiment. It should be noted that this small unit later grew by the end of the war into a regiment consisting of seventeen parachute battalions.

The letter reads:

We ought to have a corps of at least 5,000 troops, including a proportion of Australians, New Zealanders and Canadians, together with some trustworthy people from Norway and France. I see more difficulty in selecting and employing Danes, Dutch and Belgians. I hear something is being done already to form such a corps but only I believe on a very small scale. Advantage must be taken of the summer to train free forces who can, none the less, play their part meanwhile as shock troops in home defences. Pray let me have a note from the War Office on the subject.

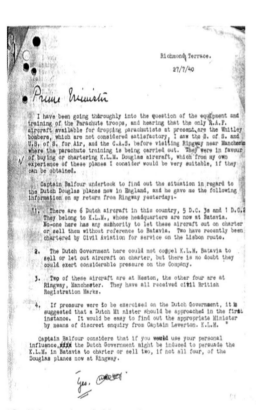

(© *Airborne Assault Museum*)   (© *Airborne Assault Museum*)

Private, No. 2 Commando

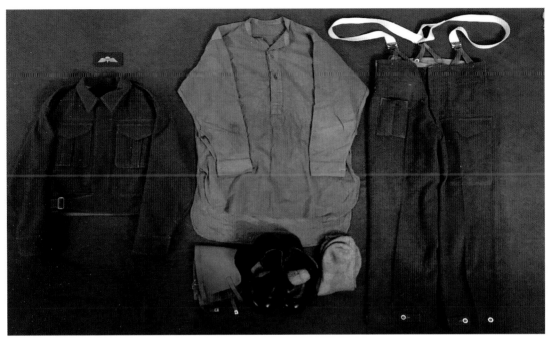

Serge battledress blouse (note unlined collar), collarless shirt, web anklets (note brass strap ends and 97 blanco), ammunition boots (initially side-laced boots similar to German *Fallschirmjäger*, then crepe-soled ammo boots), woollen socks, serge battledress trousers and white cotton braces. Just awarded un-cut Parachute Wings ready to sew on. (*Author's collection*)

An early group photo of men from No. 2 Army Commando. (*Unknown*)

Three members of 11 SAS exercising in the UK. (Note: direct copies of German paratrooper boots.) (© *Airborne Assault Museum*)

Several 'sticks', making their way out to parked aircraft. (Note: Wellington bomber with jump shield). (© *Airborne Assault Museum*)

'Chalk commander', briefing his 'stick'. (*Unknown*)

Whitley bomber dropping a 'stick' over Tatton Park, Manchester. (© *Airborne Assault Museum*)

A 'stick' of qualified parachutists. (Note: Airborne respirator haversacks.) (*Unknown*)

'High spirits'. (Note: Equipment not worn for jumping.) (© *Airborne Assault Museum*)

Chapter 2

The First Airborne Operation, 10 February 1941

olossus was the codename given to the first operation undertaken by the newly-formed British airborne forces on 10 February 1941.

The newly-formed battalion had finished its training in December 1940, and in early February 1941 thirty-eight of its members, known as X Troop, were selected to conduct an airborne operation, which was intended to test the capability of the concept of airborne troops and their equipment, as well as the ability of the Royal Air Force to accurately deliver them to the target.

The target selected for the operation was a fresh-water aqueduct near Calitri in southern Italy, that supplied water to the local population as well as several ports being used by the Italian navy. It was also considered that the destruction of the viaduct would hamper Italian military operations in Albania and North Africa. The airborne force was delivered by old Armstrong Whitworth Whitley bombers converted to drop parachutists onto the target on 10 February, but equipment failures and navigational errors meant that a significant portion of the troops' explosives in drop containers, and a team of Royal Engineer sappers, landed in the wrong area.

Early exit technique from a Whitley bomber, rapidly changed to floor exit. (© *Airborne Assault Museum*)

Dropping at Tatton Park. (© *Airborne Assault Museum*)

X Troop, No. 2 Commando, 11th SAS

(© *Airborne Assault Museum*)

Despite this setback the remaining members of the troop successfully destroyed the aqueduct and withdrew from the area, but were all captured by the Italians within a short time; their Italian translator was tortured and executed. One paratrooper managed to escape captivity, but the rest remained as prisoners of war. The aqueduct was rapidly repaired before local water reserves ran out, ensuring that the local population and the ports were not deprived of water, and, consequently, that the Italian war effort was not hampered. However, the operation served as a morale boost for the fledgling airborne forces, and the technical and operational lessons learnt assisted the further development of airborne operations.

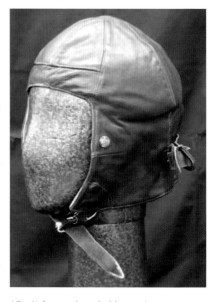

Parachuting equipment and clothing was very basic at this stage of the war. Britain was playing catch up with the German *Fallschirmjäger* formed in the late 1930s. The British parachutist smock was in effect an almost identical copy of the German one. The

(© *Airborne Assault Museum*)

initial issue of parachutist boots were also a direct copy of the German side-laced boots, but these were deemed not fit for purpose and the standard-issue ammunition boots were converted to parachutist boots by replacing the leather-studded soles with crepe rubber ones.

Minimal equipment could be carried on the person whilst parachuting. To that end most equipment and weapons less pistols and grenades were dropped with the parachutists in large containers, which were then collected once on the ground. It should also be noted the Germans had the same problem and solution at this time.

Container Light Equipment

Dropped CLE Container being recovered by Paratroopers. (© *Airborne Assault Museum*)

CLE container with parachute fitted. (© *Airborne Assault Museum*)

Group photograph of captured members of X Troop. (© *Airborne Assault Museum*)

Early photograph. (Note: Flight hats and unusual use of early Sten bandolier with SMLE rifles.) (© *Airborne Assault Museum*)

1942 Ringway and Hardwick Hall

Parachutist smock (note: almost identical to captured German parachutist smock), Sorbo rubber training helmet, collarless shirt, serge battledress blouse, early web anklets, ammo boots, woollen socks, serge battledress trousers cotton braces and Parachute wings (note uncut at this very early stage, soon cut down). (*Author's collection*)

Several 'sticks' making their way out to parked Whitley bombers. (© *Airborne Assault Museum*)

Training apparatus at Ringway. (© *Airborne Assault Museum*)

Sorbo Training Helmet

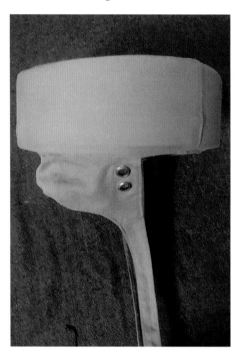 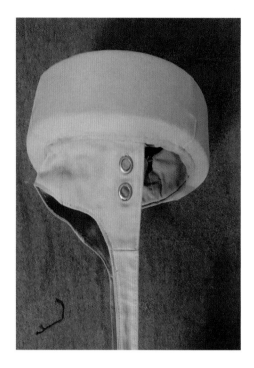

Basic cotton drill and Sorbo rubber helmet made in several variants following the same theme. Used mainly for training jumps and saw service throughout the war in this role. (*Author's collection*)

Collection of early training photographs. (© *Airborne Assault Museum*)

Whitley Bag

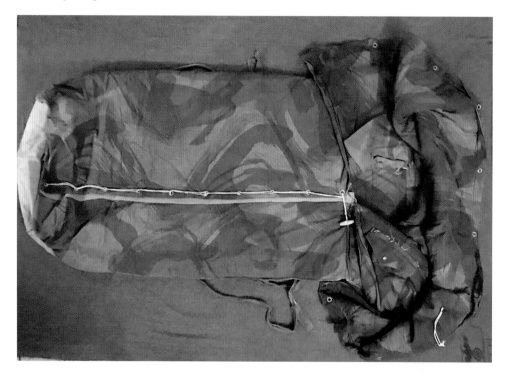

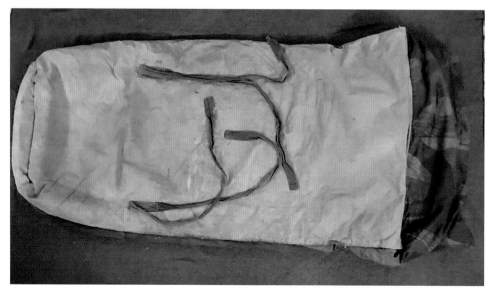

'Whitley bag', used by paratroopers to keep warm inside the bare fusilage of antiquated bombers such as the Whitley. The large V-shaped flaps were designed so they could be wrapped around the paratrooper whilst still wearing his X Type parachute. (*Author's collection*)

'Whitley bag' on the bonnet of a captured Willys Jeep during Operation Market-Garden. (© *Airborne Assault Museum*)

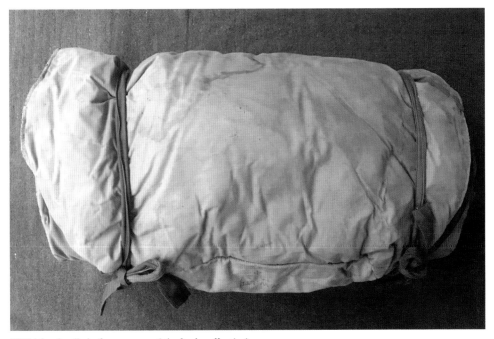

"Whitley bag" tie for stowage. (*Author's collection*)

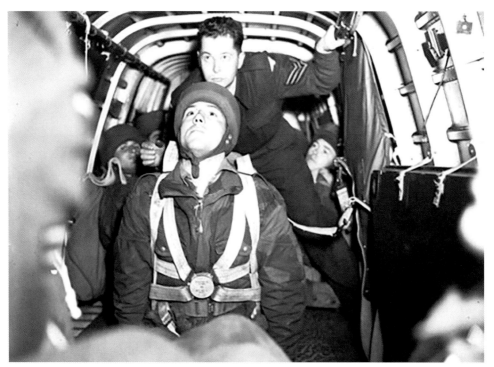

'Action stations'. Waiting for the green light. (*Unknown*)

Qualified paratroopers and aircrew next to their Whitley bomber. (© *Airborne Assault Museum*)

Early War Fighting Equipment

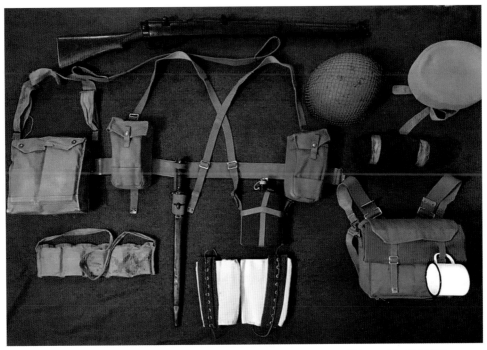

Short Magazine Lee-Enfield (SMLE) rifle, respirator, 37 Pattern webbing with SMLE bayonet, 50-round .303 ammunition bandolier, quick-release knee pads, P helmet, Sorbo rubber helmet, gas cape, small pack and tin mug. (*Author's collection*)

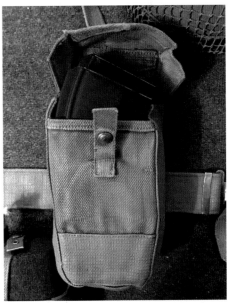

50-round .303 bandolier, two Mills grenades. (*Author's collection*)

Two Bren gun magazines. (*Author's collection*)

Early War Small Pack Contents

Small pack (blancoed KG97), early war aluminium mess tins, Tommy cookers, enamel mug, rain cape/groundsheet, boot polish and brush, woollen socks, personal tea and sugar container, issue jumper, ration bag, knife-fork-spoon (KFS), housewife, issue cellular towel and wash kit. (*Author's collection*)

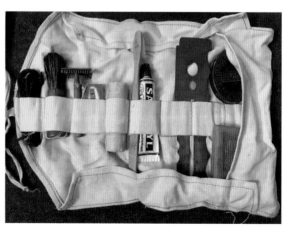

'Into action'. (© *Airborne Assault Museum*)

Exercise in the UK. (© *Airborne Assault Museum*)

Service Respirator

Two early war dark
brown gas brassards,
service respirator
haversack, service
respirator with early
war filter, anti-gas
eye shields, anti-
gas ointment in
early war container,
anti-dimming kit,
and cotton waste
for application of
ointment. (*Author's
collection*)

Parachutist Knee pads basic serge material pads, leather lace for quick removal. (*Author's collection*)

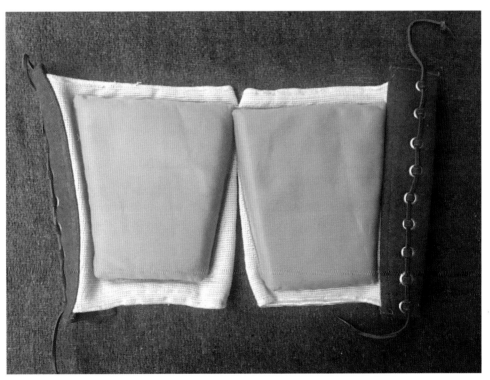

Parachutist knee pads tan cotton pads possibly use North Africa Australian made? (*Author's collection*)

Chapter 3

The Bruneval Raid, 27/28 February 1942

Operation Biting, also known as the Bruneval Raid, was a British Combined Operations raid on a German coastal radar installation at Bruneval in northern France.

On the night of 27 February 1942, after a period of intense secret training and several delays due to poor weather, 'C' Company of the 2nd Battalion The Parachute Regiment, commanded by Major John Frost, parachuted into Bruneval in France to conduct a raid to capture a newly-found German radar system that was located next to a large villa on the coast. On landing the main force was to quickly assault the villa and radar location. The radar needed to be quickly dismantled for extraction back to the Britain, where it was to be later examined by scientists trying to gain an understanding of Germany's radar capability, which was affecting the RAF's bombing efforts.

The initial assault was successful, killing several members of the immediate German garrison trying to defend and counter-attack the site. The RAF technician dropped in with the force rapidly dismantled the Würzburg radar and removed several key components. Once this had been completed the signal for the force to withdraw to the evacuation beach was given. The detachment assigned to clear the beach had initially failed to do so, but the German force guarding it was soon eliminated with the help of the main force and a returned miss-dropped party. After some 'concerned' signalling, the raiding troops were picked up by Royal Navy landing craft, also accompanied by two captured Germans, then transferred to several Motor Gun Boats which safely returned them to Britain.

The raid was entirely successful. The airborne troops suffered relatively few casualties, and the radar components they brought back, along with a captured German radar technician, allowed British scientists to understand enemy advances in radar and to create countermeasures to neutralise them.

Private, 'C' Company, 2nd Battalion The Parachute Regiment, 1st Parachute Brigade, 1st Airborne Division

P helmet, parachutist jacket, knee pads, collarless shirt, serge battledress, web anklets, ammo boots, woollen socks and early parachutist trousers. (*Author's collection*)

A member of 'C' Company's recollection of the Bruneval raid is given below:

It was a very good exit and landing, but when we came down the first thing, I noticed was that some sections and containers had gone a bit adrift. It turned out that Junior Charteris and his sections had gone down out of position and had to make a mad dash to get back and link up. We marched down to take up our positions. The main party moved up to attack the radar station, which they achieved virtually without opposition. My group was in the rear for clearing operations, mopping up pockets of German resistance, which entailed some pretty heavy skirmishes.

The only trouble was that some of our radio communications were in the containers which had gone adrift and the others that we did have were playing up. This meant that we were using runners to maintain communications with Major Frost while we were engaged with the Germans. One of the men in my party was killed as a result of the fighting and we also had a few wounded.

(© *Airborne Assault Museum*)

Unfortunately, some men got left behind and were captured. Because of the radio communications problems, when we were ready to leave, we had no contact with the Navy. John Ross fired Very lights to attract the Navy's attention. By now we had been waiting over an hour. Sergeant Major Strachan who had been wounded in the raid was beginning to feel the cold and I lent him a cricket sweater I had with me. I had brought it to keep warm in the Whitley on the flight over. Although we had dealt with the local troops there was the possibility of reinforcements arriving and a real risk of us getting onto a hiding for nothing. Fortunately, a couple of sub-lieutenants came ashore to have a look and we were taken off by assault landing craft (ALC) and transferred to gunboats. The lift off from the beach went smoothly although we did come under fire from the Germans as we were trying to get off. The radar material, wounded and prisoners were taken back by fast gunboat to Portsmouth while the rest of us remained in gunboats which accompanied the ALC's back to port. This took a pretty long time and we

(© *Airborne Assault Museum*)

were all a little sea sick by the time we eventually arrived back at Portsmouth. I am glad to say that Sergeant Major Strachan recovered but I never did get that cricket sweater back!

RAF reconnaissance photograph of the mansion at Bruneval and the Würzburg radar next to it. (© *Airborne Assault Museum*)

Commanding officer 'C' Company Major John Frost (facing the camera with helmet on). (© *Airborne Assault Museum*)

Parachutist Jacket

The parachutist jacket was effectively a direct copy of the existing German paratrooper jump smock, the only design modification being the addition of epaulettes. Another short-lived combat garment, seeing as it was superseded by the Denison smock and relegated to training use. (*Author's collection*)

Parachutist jacket made by Rego
Clothiers Ltd. (*Author's collection*)

Two members of 'C' Company photographed on one of the launches returning to the U.K. (© *Airborne Assault Museum*)

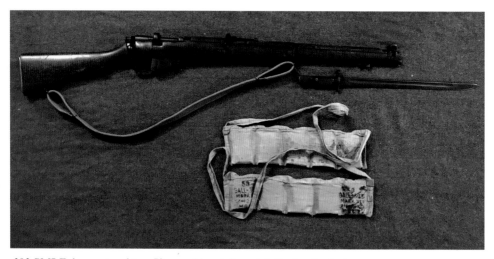

.303 SMLE, bayonet and two 50-round bandoliers. (*Author's collection*)

Parachutist Helmet

First model parachutist helmet easily identified by its distinctive flared rim at the rear. It was a very well made but complex design, hence its short issue span. It was seen worn as late as 1944 by some paratroopers in the 1st Airborne Division. The internal design was loosely copied from German paratrooper helmets of that period. (*Author's collection*)

The two captured Germans from the raid being searched and two members of 'C' Company in good spirits. (© *Airborne Assault Museum*)

Interior view of the P helmet showing manufacture stamp by BMB dated 1942. (*Author's collection*)

Parachutist standard uniform. (© *Airborne Assault Museum*)

Serge Battledress Blouse

Rare surviving serge battledress with uncut Parachutist wings and yellow cord lanyard, signifying a member of the 2nd Battalion The Parachute Regiment. (*Author's collection*)

Early Parachutist Trousers

Due to the need for parachutists to carry more equipment on the body and the lack of pockets on the early parachutist jacket, parachutist trousers were developed from standard battledress trousers by the addition of a thigh bellows pocket and straps to carry the issued commando knife. (*Author's collection*)

Royal Navy Motor launch returning Members of C Company from the raid. (© *Airborne Assault Museum*)

Continued. Flight Sergeant Cox seen in his RAF uniform and P Helmet, alongside Corporal from C Company. (© *Airborne Assault Museum*)

Chapter 4

North Africa, 1942–1943

British airborne operations in North Africa were conducted by paratroopers of the 1st Parachute Brigade, commanded by Brigadier Edwin Flavell, as part of the Tunisian campaign between November 1942 and April 1943.

When planning began for Operation Torch, the Allied invasion of North Africa in 1942, it was decided to employ the 1st Parachute Brigade, part of the 1st Airborne Division, with the Allied forces taking part, as an American airborne unit, the 2nd Battalion 509th Parachute Infantry Regiment, was also to be used during the invasion. After a short period of training and being brought up to operational strength, mainly with men from the 2nd Parachute Brigade, also part of the 1st Airborne Division, the brigade was rapidly deployed to North Africa in November 1942.

Units from the 1st Parachute Brigade conducted several jumps into Tunisia, near Bône on 12 November, then near Souk el-Arba and Béja on 13 November, and at

Members of 1st Parachute Brigade marching in Tunisia. (© *Airborne Assault Museum*)

Pont Du Fahs on 29 November, seizing airfields and then fighting as infantry after each action until an Allied armoured force linked up with them, supporting it until December 1942. Due to the inability of units of the British First Army to link up with the Pont Du Fahs force, the 2nd Parachute Battalion, under Lieutenant Colonel John Frost, was forced to withdraw over 50 miles (80km) towards the nearest Allied units. The battalion was attacked several times during the withdrawal, taking more than 250 casualties before they finally reached Allied lines.

For the next four months the 1st Parachute Brigade was used in a ground role, serving under several formations and advancing with Allied ground forces; it suffered heavy casualties on numerous occasions but also took large numbers of Axis prisoners. The brigade was transferred out of the front in mid–April 1943 and left to re-join the rest of the 1st Airborne Division to train for Operation Husky, the Allied invasion of Sicily.

The Germans gave them the nickname '*Rote Teufel*', 'Red Devils', as a sign of respect.

Captured Private Cadden of the 2nd Parachute Battalion being interrogated by German paratroopers in Tunisia.
(© *Airborne Assault Museum*)

Group of 1st Airborne paratroopers marching in Tunisia watched by former Vichy French troops.
(© *Airborne Assault Museum*)

Three officers of the 2nd Battalion resting near Beja, North Africa. (© *Airborne Assault Museum*)

Private, 2nd Battalion The Parachute Regiment, 1st Parachute Brigade, 1st Airborne Division

Two-tone scrim scarf, P helmet, first pattern Denison smock, parachutist knee pads, Aertex shirt, serge battledress blouse (2nd Battalion lanyard), web anklets, ammo boots, woollen socks and early parachutist trousers. (*Author's collection*)

Exercise in North Africa (Note: Mk 4 Lee-Enfields with spike bayonets so 1943). (© *Airborne Assault Museum*)

Commander's briefing. 'High Spirits'. (*Unknown*)

Paratrooper's Fighting Equipment, early North Africa

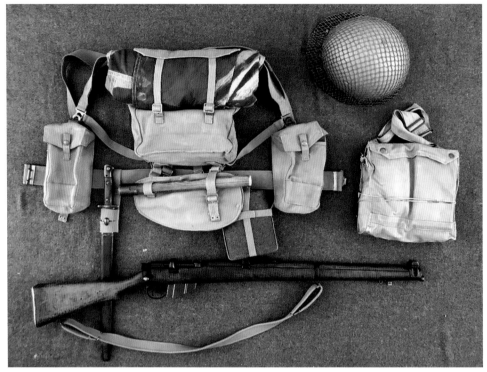

Still blancoed set of 37 Pattern webbing, SMLE of First World War vintage, P Helmet and service respirator. Note: First pattern Denison smock rolled up under small pack flap and E tool attached to bottom of the small pack. (*Author's collection*)

North Africa 1942 a group picture with local camel members of 1st Parachute battalion. (© *Airborne Assault Museum*)

Mediterranean Theatre Fighting Equipment

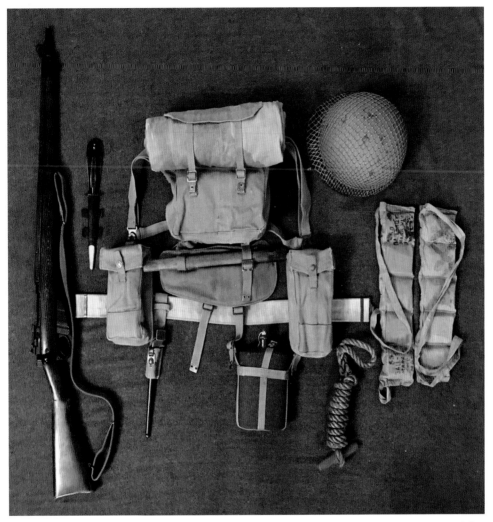

Lee Enfield Mk 4, Fairbairn–Sykes fighting knife, 37 Pattern webbing and small pack containing Denison smock, 50-round .303 ammunition bandoliers, toggle rope and P helmet. (*Author's collection*)

(© *Airborne Assault Museum*)

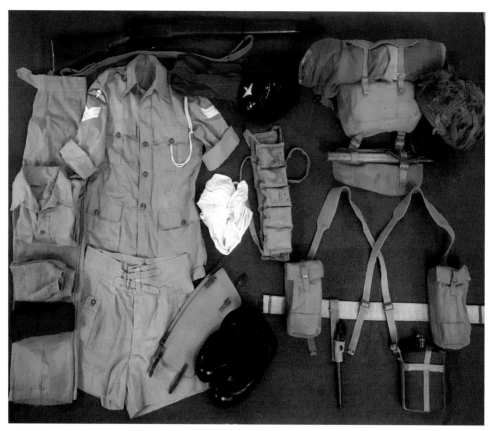

.303 Lee Enfield, khaki trousers, Aertex shirt, woollen socks, woollen hose, khaki jacket with 2nd Battalion lanyard, khaki shorts, gaiters, ammo boots, Celanese scarf, 50-round .303 bandoliers, 37 Pattern small pack with Denison smock, E-Tool, HSAT and 37 Pattern webbing. (*Author's collection*)

(© *Airborne Assault Museum*)

First Pattern Denison Smock

First pattern Denison smock dated 1942. The very first Denison smocks were made from hand-painted material pieced together. The dyes used weren't that colour-fast and quickly washed out. This added to the camouflage effect in North Africa and the Mediterranean. (*Author's collection*)

Gun group commander and Bren gunner. (© *Airborne Assault Museum*)

Advancing paratroopers 1943 (Note: Denim trousers and KD jacket.) (© *Airborne Assault Museum*)

Mepacrine Malaria Tablets

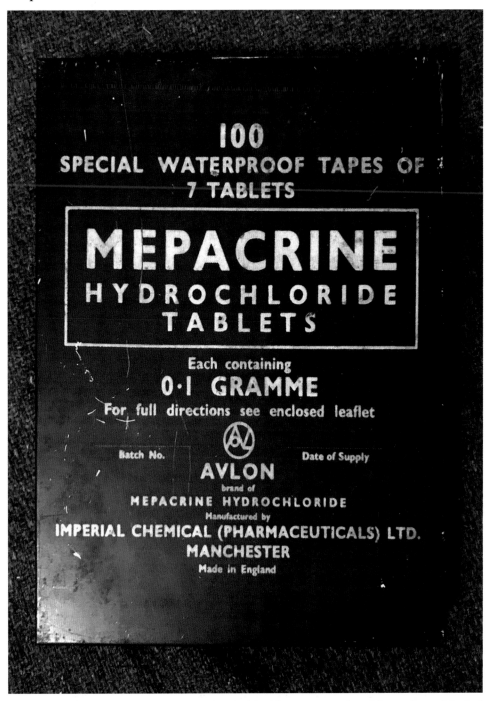

Mepacrine Hydrochloride tablets were anti-malarial tablets, very popular with members of the 2nd Parachute Battalion, hence their nicknames the 'Mepacrine Chasers'. They used them to dye their parachute cord lanyards yellow (the battalion lanyard colour). (*Author's collection*)

Correct method being used to throw Mills grenade. (© *Airborne Assault Museum*)

Projector Infantry Anti-Tank, 'PIAT', loaded and ready for action. (© *Airborne Assault Museum*)

Hot Weather KD Uniform. North Africa – Mediteranean Theatre Operations

Generic hot weather KD uniform for the North African theatre of operations. Parachute Regiment beret, Aertex head-over shirt, shorts, webbing anklets, woollen socks and ammo boots. (*Author's collection*)

Silk Escape Map

Surviving original silk escape map of North Africa and the Mediterranean, from a veteran of the 1st Airborne Division. (*Author's collection*)

Original Maps of the 1st Parachute Brigade's First Battalion Operations in the War

1st Parachute Battalion, Beja, 2nd Parachute Battalion, Oudna and 3rd Parachute Battalion, Bone. Behind are three first pattern Denison smocks and corresponding battalion insignia, alongside a P Helmet and beret. (*Author's collection*)

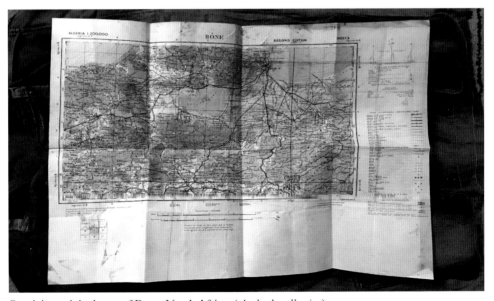

Surviving original map of Bone, North Africa. (*Author's collection*)

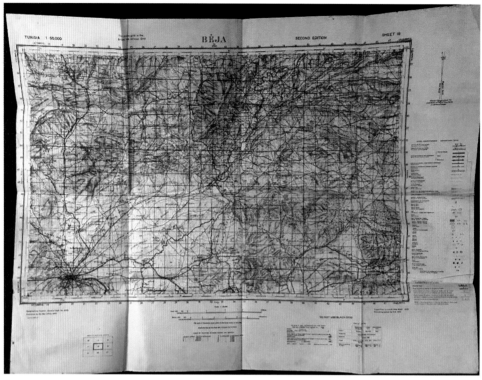

Original map of Beja. (*Author's collection*)

Original surviving map
of Oudna 2nd Parachute
Battalion. (*Author's
collection*)

Chapter 5

Operation Fustian, Sicily–Italy 1943

(© *Airborne Assault Museum*)

Operation Fustian was an airborne forces operation undertaken during the Allied invasion of Sicily in July 1943, carried out by Brigadier Gerald Lathbury's 'battle-hardened' 1st Parachute Brigade, part of the British 1st Airborne Division. Their objective was the Primosole Bridge across the Simeto River. The intention was for the brigade, with glider-borne forces in support, to land on both sides of the river. They would then capture the bridge and secure the surrounding area until relieved by the advance of British XIII Corps, which had landed on the south-eastern coast three days previously. Because the bridge was the only crossing on the river that would give the British Eighth Army access to the Catania plain, its capture was vital and expected to speed the advance and lead to the defeat of the Axis forces in Sicily.

Many of the aircraft carrying the paratroopers from North Africa were shot down or were damaged and turned back by friendly fire from the Navy and enemy action. Evasive action taken by the pilots scattered the brigade over a large area and only the equivalent of two companies of troops were landed in the correct locations. Despite this and the defence by German and Italian forces, the British paratroopers captured the bridge then repulsed all attacks and held out against increasing odds until nightfall. The relief force led by the 50th (Northumbrian) Infantry Division, under Major-General Sidney C. Kirkman, which was short of transport, were still 1 mile (1.6km) away when they halted for the night. By this time, with casualties mounting and supplies running short, Lathbury was forced to relinquish control of the bridge to the German/Italian forces. The following day the British units joined forces and the 9th Battalion, Durham Light Infantry, with tank support, attempted to recapture the bridge. The bridge was not finally secured until three days after the start of the operation, when another battalion of the Durham Light Infantry, led by the surviving paratroopers, established a bridgehead on the north bank of the river.

The capture of Primosole Bridge did not provide the expected rapid advance, due to the time it took to take which allowed the Germans to gather their forces and established a strong defensive line. It was not until early in the following month that the Eighth Army captured Catania. By the end of the operation the surviving members of the 1st Parachute Brigade had been withdrawn to Malta and took no further part in the conquest of Sicily. Lessons were again learned from the operation and were put into practice in further Allied airborne operations.

Parachute Regiment Soldier's Clothing and Equipment – Operation Fustian, Primosole Bridge

Denim trousers, .303 Lee-Enfield, cotton underwear, Parachute Regiment beret, 37 Pattern webbing (note the haversack has the shovel attached to the bottom), two 50-round .303 ammunition bandoliers, scrim scarf, Angola wool shirt, Celanese signal panel, ammo boots, web anklets and woollen socks. (*Author's collection*)

Model for the upcoming Operation Husky drop into Sicily. (© *Airborne Assault Museum*)

Chapter 6

Italy 1943

In September 1943, the 4th, 5th and 6th Battalions (2nd Parachute Brigade) and the 10th, 11th and 156th Battalions (4th Parachute Brigade) took part in Operation Slapstick, a landing from the sea near the port of Taranto in Italy.

Their objective was to capture the port and several nearby airfields and link up with the British Eighth Army, before pressing north to join the US Fifth Army near Foggia. They landed unopposed on 9 September 1943, but fifty-eight men of the 6th Battalion were lost at sea when their ship struck a mine. Pushing inland, the paratroopers captured the town of Castellaneta and the town and airfield of Gioia Del Colle before the 4th Parachute Brigade was withdrawn from the theatre.

Members of 4th Parachute Brigade administrating themselves next to their primitive accommodation. (Note: Thompson sub-machine gun). (© *Airborne Assault Museum*)

On 14 September 1943, a company of the 11th Battalion carried out a parachute drop on the island of Kos. The Italian garrison surrendered, and the company was quickly reinforced by men from the 1st Battalion, Durham Light Infantry and the Royal Air Force Regiment, before being withdrawn on 25 September and in December 1943, the 11th Battalion then re-joined the division in England.

The 2nd Parachute Brigade fought on in Italy under command of several infantry divisions, including the 2nd New Zealand Division and 8th Indian Infantry Division. In June 1944 they carried out Operation Hasty, the only parachute drop on the Italian mainland. This was a sixty-man raid ahead of 2nd NZ Division's area intended to disrupt the German demolition plan during the withdrawal from the Gothic Line. 2nd Parachute Brigade took part in Operation Dragoon in southern France, then returned to Italy briefly before being sent to Greece.

'Landings' compliments of the Royal Navy. (© *Airborne Assault Museum*)

'Filing down' self-cast newly-authorised Parachute Regiment cap badge.
(© *Airborne Assault Museum*)

M28A1 Thompson Sub-machine Gun

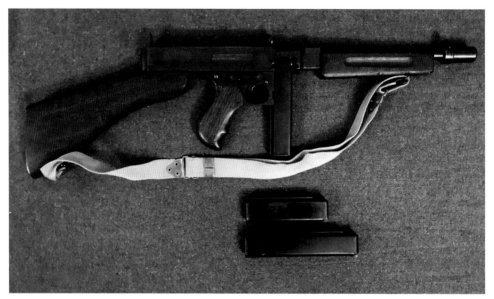

M28A1 Thompson sub-machine gun, 20-round magazine, 30-round magazine. (*Author's collection*)

Thompson sub-machine
gun being carried by
a paratrooper in Italy.
(*Unknown*)

'Some time out'.
(Note the wet, muddy
conditions.) (*Unknown*)

3in mortar crew.
(© *Airborne Assault
Museum*)

Chapter 7

Operation Simcol, Italy 1943

D uring the battles for Italy huge numbers of Allied prisoners of war held by the Italians had managed to escape from their camps into the neighbouring hills and countryside before the Germans had time to move in and reassert control over them.

An operation to rescue and evacuate personnel in the Marche and Abruzzi regions was planned in mid-September by 15 Army Group, over fears that German forces would quickly take steps to recapture the escaped prisoners then immediately transport them to Germany away from the approaching Allied forces.

It was imperative the operation should be conducted as quickly as possible and detailed planning was started by Lieutenant Colonel Simmonds at Bari on 29 September 1943. It was considered that 2 October was the earliest date by which all aircraft and stores could be assembled for the operation.

The plan required five 'sticks' of men to drop into different areas and co-ordinate the rescue operation with jeep patrols from 2 Special Air Service Regiment (2 SAS) assisting. Each 'stick' was planned to comprise one officer, an interpreter and eight other ranks. Three detachments were provided by 1st Parachute Brigade, one from each of the battalions, another was provided by 2 SAS and the fifth by US forces.

Each detachment was tasked to seek out the escaped prisoners of war and send them to a designated rendezvous location where they were to be extracted by chartered Italian vessels or Assault Landing Craft (ALCs) carrying British armed guards and taken back to Termoli.

All briefings and final arrangements were made in Bari, on 30 September and 1 October the detachments were issued with local money, maps, escape aid boxes and cigarettes.

The 'sticks' dropped with rations for only 48 hours, Sten guns, ammunition and grenades. It was planned that re-supply Dakota aircraft would drop further supplies in support of the search and rescue parties. Incredibly not all the detachments had signal equipment due to a shortage of wireless sets.

The operation was planned to last no longer than 14 days. Incredibly most men who took part in Operation Simcol remained behind enemy lines for much longer than this. After 15 November 1943 all the members of 1st Parachute

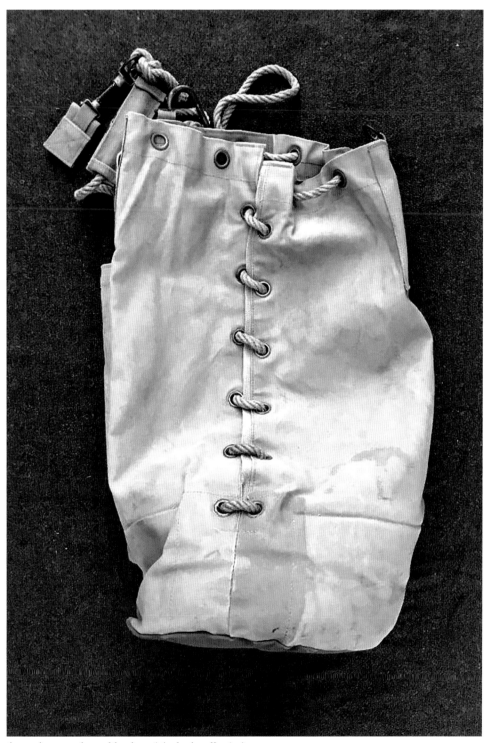

An early tan-coloured leg bag. (*Author's collection*)

Battalion's detachment and most of 2nd Parachute Battalion's detachment were unaccounted for.

The mission was extremely hazardous for the members of the Simcol detachments, due to German forces following Hitler's infamous 'Commando Order' issued on 18 October 1942, ordering the execution of all men operating on Commando raids against German troops regardless of circumstances.

(*Unknown*)

Early Fibre Rim HSAT

Early fibre rim Helmet Steel Airborne Troops (HSAT), with stitched chinstraps and economy-measure liner using felt and rubber padding. (*Author's collection*)

Chapter 8

The Battle of Kos, 14/15 September 1943

With the capitulation of Italy in September 1943, German forces in the Balkans and the Mediterranean rapidly moved to take over Italian-held areas. At the same time, the Allies, on the orders of Churchill, endeavoured to occupy the Dodecanese island chain. Under Italian control since 1912, these islands were strategically located in the south-eastern Aegean Sea, and Churchill hoped to use them as a base against German positions in the Balkans, and to pressure the neutral country of Turkey into joining the Allies.

The main objective, the island of Rhodes, had fallen to a swift attack by a German mechanized brigade. However, British forces had now landed on several islands, most notably Kos and Leros, and together with the now-friendly Italian forces located their future aspirations could now be focused to eventually retake Rhodes. On 13 September 1943 thirty-eight Liberators bombers from North Africa bombed the three airfields on the island of Rhodes, effectively grounding the Luftwaffe aircraft there, while units of the Special Boat Squadron (SBS) landed on Kos, occupying the port and the airfield near the village of Antimachia. On 14 September two Beaufighters and several Spitfires from 7 Squadron South African Airforce (SAAF) flew in to the now-captured airfield. On the night of the 14/15 September 120 paratroopers from 11th Parachute Battalion were dropped by Dakotas of No. 216 Squadron RAF on the island. The paratroopers were welcomed on the dropping zone by the Italian garrison.

At first light on 15 September, a standing patrol of two Spitfires of No. 7 SAAF Squadron was maintained over Kos to give cover to the transport aircraft and ships bringing stores and reinforcements. Among these were the first troops of the RAF Regiment who flew from the British Mandate of Palestine with nine 20mm Hispano-Suiza HS.404 guns for anti-aircraft defence of the airfield, followed two days later by a second detachment, which brought up to strength one of the first of the Regiment's squadrons to be transported to the battlefield by air with all its weapons.

On the ground, the Allied force consisted of the 1st Battalion, Durham Light Infantry, a company from 11th Parachute Battalion of 1st Airborne Division, a company of men from the SBS and Royal Air Force (RAF) personnel under the command of Lieutenant Colonel L.R.F. Kenyon. The force totalled 1,600 British (although only 1,115 were combatants, 880 army and 235 from the RAF Regiment) and about 3,500 Italian servicemen from the original garrison.

Group picture of paratroopers belonging to the 1st Airborne Division. (*Unknown*)

First Pattern Denison Smocks

Left: 1943 camouflage-printed first pattern Denison smock. Right: 1942 hand-brushed camouflage first pattern Denison. (*Author's collection*)

Group photograph of members of the 1st Battalion and attachments prior to the Market-Garden drop. (Note smock sizes). (© *Airborne Assault Museum*)

Chapter 9

Training in the United Kingdom, 1944

Corporal, 2nd Battalion The Parachute Regiment, 1st Parachute Brigade, 1st Airborne Division

Serge battledress blouse with 2nd Parachute Battalion insignia, anklets, woollen socks, beret, battledress trousers, 37 Pattern webbing belt, issue collarless shirt and woollen underwear. (*Author's collection*)

9th Parachute Battalion Training in Britain

The battalion's first commanding officer was Lieutenant Colonel James Hill. His first order on being appointed was to send the entire battalion on a forced march, at the end of which he announced that the battalion would 'work a six and a half day week' with Sunday afternoons off, until it was well-trained and fit. The battalion was assigned to the 3rd Parachute Brigade, which was initially attached to the 1st Airborne Division, but in April 1943 the 1st Airborne Division departed for the Mediterranean and the Allied invasion of Sicily without the 3rd Parachute Brigade. On 23 April 9th Parachute Battalion and the brigade were transferred to the newly-formed 6th Airborne Division. At the same time Hill was promoted to take over as the brigade commander and he was replaced as commanding officer by Lieutenant Colonel Terrance Otway. By 1944 a headquarters or support company, was added to the battalion. It comprised five platoons: motor transport, signals, mortar, machine-gun and anti-tank, armed with eight 3in mortars, four Vickers machine guns and ten PIAT anti-tank projectors.

All members of the battalion had to undergo a twelve-day parachute training course carried out at No. 1 Parachute Training School, RAF Ringway. Initial parachute jumps were from a converted barrage balloon and finished with five parachute jumps from an aircraft. Anyone failing to complete a descent was returned to his old unit. Those men who successfully completed the parachute course were presented with their maroon beret and parachute wings.

Airborne soldiers were expected to fight against superior numbers of the enemy, armed with heavy weapons, including artillery and tanks. Hence, training was designed to encourage a spirit of self-discipline, self-reliance and aggressiveness. Emphasis was given to physical fitness, marksmanship and fieldcraft. A large part of the training regime consisted of assault courses and route marching. Military exercises included capturing and holding airborne bridgeheads, road or railway bridges and coastal fortifications. At the end of most exercises, the battalion would march back to their barracks. An ability to cover long distances at speed was expected: airborne platoons were required to cover a distance of 50 miles (80km) in 24 hours, and battalions 32 miles (51km).

Parachute Regiment Insignia of the 1st Airborne Division June 1944

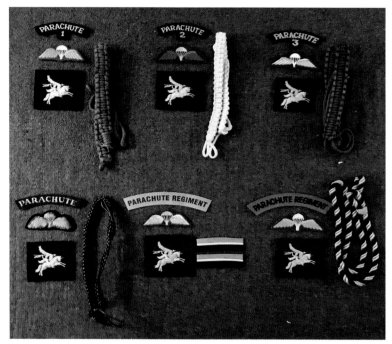

1st Parachute Brigade consisting of 1st Parachute Battalion (green lanyard), 2nd Parachute Battalion (yellow lanyard), 3rd Parachute Battalion (red lanyard).

4th Parachute Brigade consisting of 156th Parachute Battalion (black lanyard and black-backed wings), 10th Parachute Battalion (navy blue, orange, light blue epaulettes), 11th Parachute Battalion (navy blue and light blue lanyard). (*Author's collection*)

Members of the 2nd Parachute Battalion wearing their distinctive yellow lanyards. (*R. Hilton*)

Parachute Battalions Insignia of the 6th Airborne Division June 1944

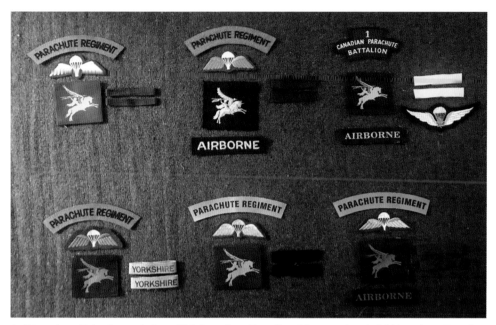

3rd Parachute Brigade consisting of 8th Parachute Battalion (blue epaulette), 9th Parachute Battalion (red epaulette), 1st Canadian Parachute Battalion (yellow epaulette).
5th Parachute Brigade consisting of 12th Parachute Battalion (light blue epaulette with YORKSHIRE), 13th Parachute Battalion (black epaulette), 7th Parachute Battalion (green epaulette). Note: The 7th Parachute Battalion left the 3rd Parachute Brigade to join the 5th Parachute Brigade on 11 August 1943. (*Author's collection*)

A sergeant of one of the parachute battalions in 6th Airborne Division displaying coloured epaulette tab. (*Unknown*)

Royal visit by Queen Elizabeth and her daughter Princess Elizabeth (the future Queen). (© *Airborne Assault Museum*)

CLE canister post–
drop being unpacked
and paratroopers
assembling a Welbike
lightweight folding
motorcycle.
(© *Airborne Assault
Museum*)

Private, 12th Battalion The Parachute Regiment, 5th Parachute Brigade, 6th Airborne Division

Austerity battledress blouse showing insignia of 12th Parachute Battalion, anklets, ammo boots woollen socks, beret, austerity battledress trousers, 37 Pattern belt, issue shirt and woollen underwear. (*Author's collection*)

12th Parachute Battalion Training in Britain

In May 1943, the 10th (East Riding Yeomanry) Battalion, Green Howards was converted to parachute duties, becoming the 12th (Yorkshire) Parachute Battalion, under the command of Lieutenant Colonel R.G. Parker. The battalion was then assigned to the 5th Parachute Brigade, part of the 6th Airborne Division.

Upon formation, the battalion had an establishment of 556 men in three rifle companies. The companies were divided into a small headquarters and three platoons. The platoons had three Bren guns and three 2in mortars, one of each per section. The only heavy weapons in the battalion were a 3in mortar and a Vickers machine gun platoon. By 1944 a headquarters or support company was added to the battalion.

Group photograph of paratroopers from the 6th Airborne Division (Note: new Airborne insignia being worn.) (© *Airborne Assault Museum*)

His Majesty King George VI inspecting members of the 10th Parachute Battalion. (© *Airborne Assault Museum*)

37 Pattern Webbing Non-Commissioned Officer armed with Sten Mk V

Sten Mk V, 37 Pattern standard fighting order with the addition of the Sten bayonet frog containing retaining plate for the Sten's working parts when stripped down for parachute descent. Small pack showing ground sheet stowed under main flap and a gas cape attached to the bottom of the pack. (*Author's collection*)

Ammunition carried in the Rifleman's Pouches

Left-hand pouch containing bandolier with 50 rounds of .303 rifle ammunition and two Mills grenades. Right-hand pouch containing, two Bren gun magazines. (*Author's collection*)

Chapter 10

Operation Hasty, Italy, June 1944

O peration Hasty was a mission behind German lines in Italy. It was carried out in June 1944, by a small force of sixty men drawn from the 2nd (Independent) Parachute Brigade. Their objective was to land behind German positions in the Abruzzo region near Trassaco and interdict supply lines and the movement of troops as they withdrew from Sora to Avezzano.

The detachment took off from Guado Airfield at 19:00 on 1 June 1944, in three Douglas Dakota aircraft accompanied by another eight aircraft belonging to an American squadron carrying dummy parachutists. The aircraft reached the drop zone near Trasaco by 20:30, and the landing was successful with only one casualty, a paratrooper with a broken rib. At 21:00 the force had assembled at their rendezvous and radio contact was established with the 2nd New Zealand Infantry Division who were in overall command of the mission and arrangements were made for the planned resupply parachute drops to go ahead. The detachment commander established a patrol base and the detachment was divided into three patrols each commanded by an officer.

German reaction to the landing was swift and their reconnaissance patrols were in the area within 20 minutes and the British base located and attacked within 24 hours. Avoiding a pitched battle, the three patrols split up and for the next seven days disrupted German convoys and demolition parties. In response to the British presence a German brigade was detailed to locate the force and a division was held back in reserve instead of moving to reinforce the front line. During their search for the paratroopers, the Germans captured the detachment's signallers and radio contact with the New Zealand division was lost when the detachment's sole remaining radio was damaged.

By 7 June it was decided to withdraw the detachment, but with no radio working there was no way to pass on the decision. The 2nd Parachute Brigade commander, Brigadier Pritchard, then came up with the idea of dropping leaflets around the area with the message 'Proceed Awdry forthwith'. The message meant little to the Germans, but the British knew that Captain Awdry was the 6th Parachute Battalion's liaison officer assigned to the 2nd New Zealand Division. The detachment then split up into smaller groups and attempted to make their own way back to the Allied lines.

Of the sixty men involved in Operation Hasty, only two officers and twenty-five men successfully returned to Allied lines. Little physical or material damage was caused to the Germans, but a small measure of success was the diversion of a brigade to hunt down sixty men and the tying-down of a division retained behind the front line during the mission. The Germans succeeded in withdrawing to the Gothic Line, and held the Allies there until mid-September when, after the Battle of Rimini, the city was captured.

(© *Airborne Assault Museum*)

Although Hasty was one of only two British airborne operations on mainland Italy during the war, the 2nd Parachute Brigade went on to carry out two bigger airborne operations involving the whole brigade later the same year. In August they participated in Operation Dragoon, the invasion of the South of France, and in October, Operation Manna in Greece.

Fibre Rim Helmet Steel Airborne Troops (HSAT)

Fibre rim HSAT with common later copper rivet-joined chinstraps and full rubber-padded liner. (*Author's collection*)

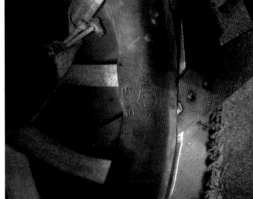

Interior of later fibre rim HSAT dated 1943. (*Author's collection*)

Chapter 11

D-Day, 6 June 1944

Operation Overlord was the code name for the invasion of Normandy, the Allied operation that launched the successful liberation of German-occupied Western Europe. The operation was due to be launched on 4 June 1944, but bad weather postponed the invasion by 24 hours.

On the evening of 5 June 1944 up to 1,500 aircraft flew the 13,000 soldiers of the American 82nd and 101st Divisions alongside 7,000 British paratroopers and glider soldiers from the 6th Airborne Division into the night skies over Normandy. 22nd Independent Parachute Company pathfinders marked the British drop zones.

The 6th Airborne Division faced marginal winds and heavy German flak widely scattered the drop so that only 40 per cent of the division could form up for its initial tasks. The coup de main glider assault on the Orne River and Canal bridges was totally successful. Despite only gathering 150 of the 600-plus men commanded by Lieutenant Colonel Otway, the 9th Parachute Battalion assaulted the Merville Gun Battery, storming it with what he had assembled at the battalion rendezvous. They managed to occupy it, but lost half the assaulting force. The bridges across the Dives River were destroyed on time. Savage scattered fighting broke out over the 24 square miles of enemy territory the division was required to hold, as isolated and often leaderless bands of paratroopers fought on regardless. German forces who would otherwise have been directed against the invasion beachhead were tied down.

By the end of D-Day seaborne commandos and infantry relieved the coup de main party reinforced by 7 Para at 'Pegasus Bridge' on the Orne River. Also, much needed glider-borne infantry from 6th Airlanding Brigade arrived that evening.

Four days later the Germans attempted to push through the airborne sector protecting the invasion beaches at the small town of Breville. Counter-attacks by German infantry supported by tanks were beaten off in a fierce two-day battle that raged back and forth. Breville was finally captured by the paratroopers and held but at enormous cost, thereby saving the invasion from faltering.

Fighting increased throughout June and July with the division engaged in intense fighting to hold the eastern flank of the Normandy bridgehead. In August the division participated in the general Allied breakout to the River Seine.

The 6th Airborne Division was not withdrawn from the fighting until 27 August, having spent 82 days in non-stop action in the front line. Losses were horrendous, with 542 killed, 1,623 wounded and 725 missing. Almost one man in five was a casualty.

Pathfinders prior to the Normandy drop. (© *Airborne Assault Museum*)

Sergeant, 9th Battalion The Parachute Regiment, 3rd Parachute Brigade, 6th Airborne Division

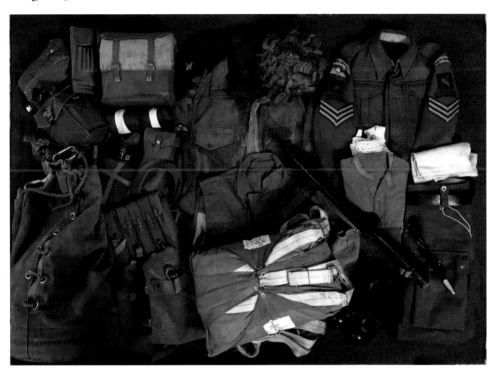

37 Pattern webbing, blancoed KG3, 37 Pattern small pack with groundsheet attached and gas cape, lightweight respirator haversack and toggle rope, leg bag, Sten bandolier, parachutist life vest, X Type parachute, parachutist jacket, later pattern 1st model Denison smock, scrim scarf, maroon beret and Parachute Regiment cap badge, HSAT fibre rim, serge battledress blouse with insignia for the 9th Battalion The Parachute Regiment, 6th Airborne Division, string vest, collarless shirt, woollen underwear, parachutist trousers, web anklets, Sten Mk V, Fairbairn-Sykes knife, woollen socks and ammunition boots. (*Author's collection*)

Paratroopers of the 6th Airborne Division 'camming up' prior to the Normandy drop. (© *Airborne Assault Museum*)

Stirling towing a Horsa glider on take off. (© *Airborne Assault Museum*)

Paratroopers moving through wrecked town. (© *Airborne Assault Museum*)

Private, Canadian Parachute Battalion, 3rd Parachute Brigade, 6th Airborne Division

37 Pattern webbing, blancoed KG3, 37 small pack with groundsheet attached and gas cape, lightweight respirator haversack and toggle rope, leg bag, parachutist life vest, X Type parachute, Lee-Enfield Mk 4, rifle drop valise, parachutist jacket, later pattern 2nd model Denison smock, maroon beret and Canadian Parachute Regiment cap badge, fibre rim HSAT, Canadian serge battledress blouse with insignia for the 1st Canadian Parachute Battalion, 6th Airborne Division, string vest, collarless shirt, woollen underwear, British parachutist trousers, Fairbairn–Sykes knife, woollen socks and US Corcoran jump boots. (*Author's collection*)

Canadian paratroopers of the 6th Airborne Division (Note: US Corcoran jump boots.) (*Unknown*)

Canadian paratroopers dug in, manning a Bren gun. (*Unknown*)

A good view of a
Canadian paratrooper
sergeant's insignia.
(*Unknown*)

6th Airborne Division Uniform

Canadian Denison smock, Canadian blouse, glider pilot blouse, 7th Battalion blouse, Para beret, HSATs, 8th Battalion Denison smock, 9th Battalion blouse and 12th Battalion blouse. (*Author's collection*)

A group of 'cheerful' paratroopers at Ranville in Normandy. (© *Airborne Assault Museum*)

Glider Pilot Regiment

Glider pilot flight helmet, Glider Pilot Regiment staff sergeant's austerity blouse, first pattern Denison smock and regimental cap badge. After landing their gliders the men of the Glider Pilot Regiment fought alongside their passengers and the paratroopers. (*Author's collection*)

Second model rucksack, 37 Pattern webbing with assault gas mask, .303 ammunition bandoliers, HSAT, Denison smock, toggle rope, torch, binoculars, map case, glider pilot helmet, flight goggles, mask, scrim scarf, beret, Glider Pilot Regiment austerity blouse, battledress trousers, collarless shirt, string vest, underwear, collarless shirt and anklets. (*Author's collection*)

Glider Pilots receiving pre flight brief.
(© *Airborne Assault Museum*)

Horsa glider on landing zone in Normandy.
(© *Airborne Assault Museum*)

Late War Rucksack

Second model rucksack commonly used by the Glider Pilot Regiment. (*Author's collection*)

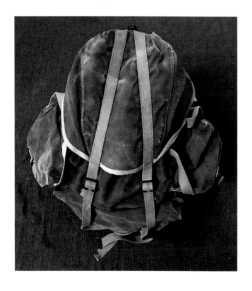

Parachuting Equipment

Leg bag (used for dropping equipment with the man), rifle valise, second model X Type parachute, first model X Type, and parachutist jacket (worn over equipment, to prevent rigging lines snagging). (*Author's collection*)

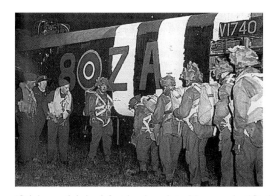

'Sticks explaining' for the drop into Normandy. (© *Airborne Assault Museum*)

Rifle Valise

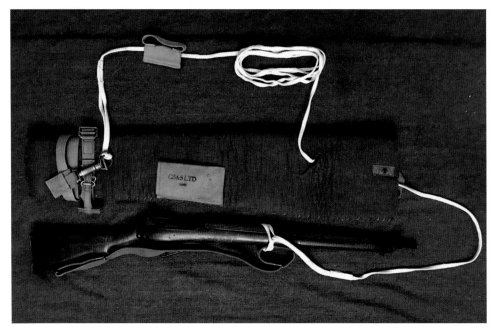

The drop line was attached to the rifle by passing it through the sling behind the swivel. (*Author's collection*)

The drop line was then prepared for stowage, by wrapping it around the pocket. (*Author's collection*)

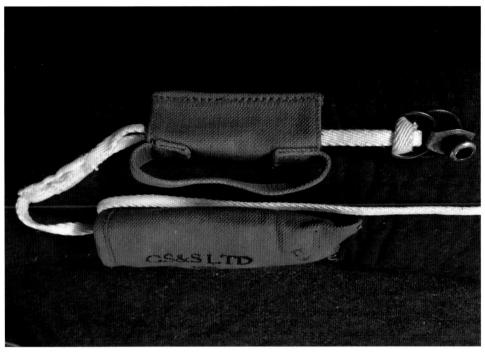

The drop line was then stowed in the pocket. (*Author's collection*)

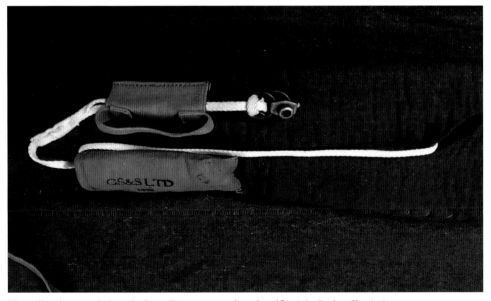

Note: line is passed though the valise connected to the rifle. (*Author's collection*)

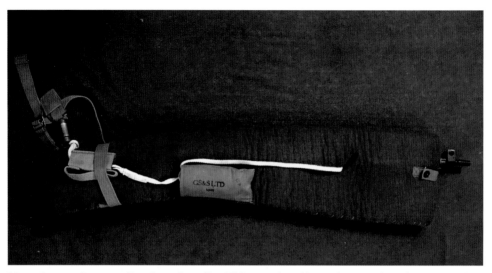

Note: the muzzle protruding from the valise. This was placed into a bayonet frog that was attached to the parachutist anklet. (*Author's collection*)

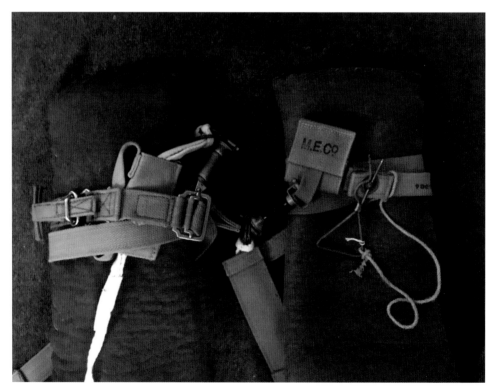

Later rifle valise release system (toggle). Earlier rifle valise release system (wire pin). (*Author's collection*)

Briefing paratroopers of the 6th Airborne Division prior to Operation Overlord. (© *Airborne Assault Museum*)

Rifleman Oxf Bucks Light Infantry, Air landing brigade

Mk 4 Lee Enfield rifle, Gammon bomb, Hawkins mine, Helmet Airborne Troops, 37 Pattern webbing (note: bayonet fitted to shoulder strap and small pack fitted to lower straps, 303 ammunition bandoliers, Maroon beret Oxf Bucks insignia, Denison smock, scrim scarf, toggle rope, Battledress blouse with Oxf Bucks insignia, Battledress trousers, collarless shirt, underwear, socks and anklets.

Parachutist/Airborne Life Vest

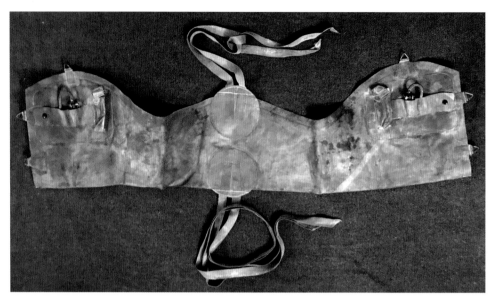

Parachutist life vest used by both paratroopers and glider-borne troops. (*Author's collection*)

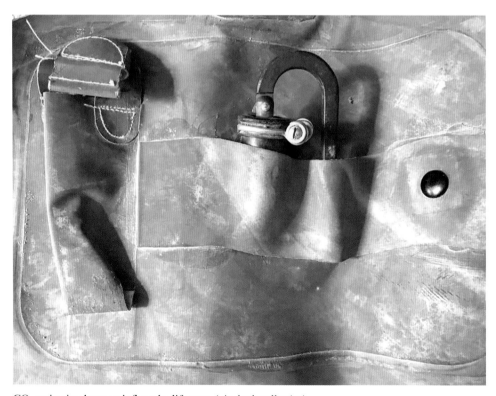

CO_2 activation lever to inflate the life vest. (*Author's collection*)

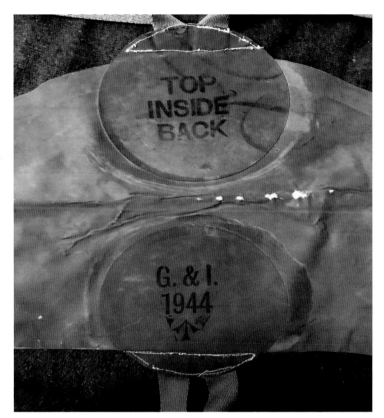

Parachutist life vest
markings dated 1944.
(*Author's collection*)

Paratroopers emplaning for the Normandy drop. (© *Airborne Assault Museum*)

Fantastic
photograph of
a paratrooper
getting ready to
'Go to it'.
(© *Airborne
Assault Museum*)

Parachutists aboard a Stirling bomber ready for the Normandy drop. (© *Airborne Assault Museum*)

Helmet Steel Airborne Troops Steel Band

The fibre rim was replaced, and the edge of the HSAT was simplified with the addition of a steel rim band. (*Author's collection*)

Chapter 12

Operation Dragoon, Southern France 1944

O peration Dragoon (initially Operation Anvil) was the code name for the Allied invasion of southern France on 15 August 1944. The operation was initially to take place in conjunction with Operation Overlord, the Allied landing in Normandy, but a lack of resources led to the cancellation of the second landing. By July 1944 the landing was reconsidered, as the ports of Normandy did not have the capacity to adequately supply Allied forces. As a result, the operation was finally approved in July to be carried in August.

The objective of the operation was for the Allies to secure the vital ports on the French Mediterranean coast and increase pressure on German forces by opening a second front. After some preliminary commando operations, including the British 2nd Para's landing behind enemy lines to secure vital transport links, the US VI Corps landed on the beaches of the Côte d'Azur under the cover of a large naval task force, followed by several divisions of the French Armee 'B'. They were opposed by the scattered forces of German Army Group G, weakened by the relocation of its divisions to other fronts and the replacement of many of its soldiers with third-rate *Ost-Bataillone*, made up of Eastern European ex-prisoners of war and deserters and outfitted with obsolete equipment.

Hindered by Allied air superiority and a large-scale uprising by the French Resistance, the degraded German forces were swiftly defeated. They withdrew to the north through the Rhône valley, to establish a fairly stable defence line at Dijon. Allied mobile units overtook the Germans and partially blocked their route at Montélimar. The ensuing battle led to a stalemate, with neither side able to achieve a decisive breakthrough, until the Germans were finally able to complete their withdrawal and retreat from the town. While the Germans were retreating, the French captured the important ports of Marseille and Toulon, putting them into operation soon afterwards.

The Germans were not able to hold Dijon and ordered a complete withdrawal from southern France. Army Group G retreated further north, pursued by Allied forces. The fighting ultimately came to a stop at the Vosges mountains, where Army Group G was finally able to establish a stable defensive line. The Allied forces needed reorganizing and, facing stiffened German resistance, the offensive was halted on 14 September. Operation Dragoon was considered a success by the Allies. It enabled them to liberate most of southern France in only four weeks, while inflicting heavy casualties on the enemy, although many of the best German units were able to escape. The captured French ports were put into operation, allowing the Allies to improve their supply situation.

2nd Parachute Brigade Insignia

2nd Parachute Brigade consisting of 4th Parachute Battalion (black lanyard), 5th Parachute Battalion (Hunting Stewart tartan patch behind cap badge), and 6th Parachute Battalion (black collar ribbon). (*Author's collection*)

Invasion armband with Union Flag. (*Author's collection*)

British and US paratroopers relaxing together in southern France. (© *Airborne Assault Museum*)

A British paratrooper out of combat taking time to get a picture. (*Unknown*)

Private 6th Battalion The Parachute Regiment, 2nd Independent Parachute Brigade

Scrim scarf, parachute neck scarf (cut from parachute canopy), fighting equipment, Thompson sub-machine gun, Aertex shirt, parachutist trousers, Fairbairn-Sykes knife, first pattern Denison smock, ammo boots, woollen socks, gaiters, Mills grenades, Gammon bomb and Hawkins mine. (*Author's collection*)

Bren gun position. (© *Airborne Assault Museum*)

Paratroopers aboard a Dakota. (Note: Union Flag armband.) (© *Airborne Assault Museum*)

Drop going into southern France. (© *Airborne Assault Museum*)

WS38 Section Level Radio Set

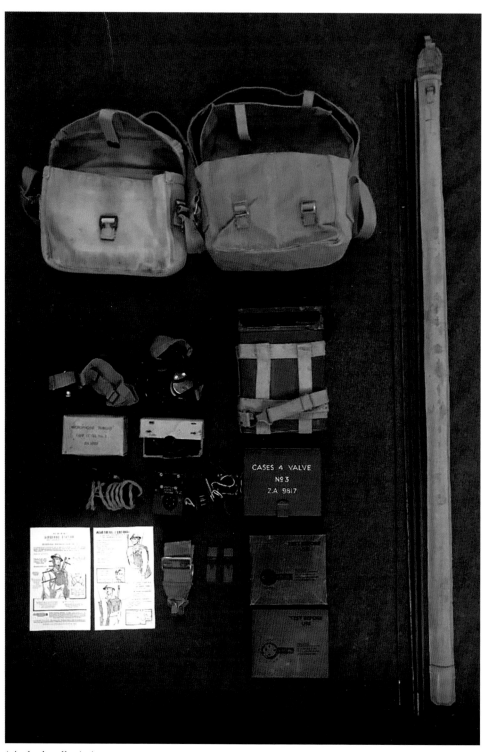

(Author's collection)

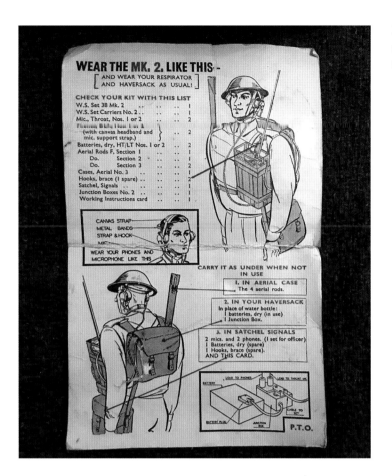

Instruction card for the WS38 radio. (*Author's collection*)

Face of the WS38 radio. (*Author's collection*)

Parachutist signaller correctly carrying a
WS38 set. (*Unknown*)

Another photograph of a parachutist
signaller correctly carrying a WS38 set.
(*Unknown*)

Good photograph of paratroopers landing. (© *Airborne Assault Museum*)

Two paratroopers from the 5th Parachute Battalion 'sightseeing'. (© *Airborne Assault Museum*)

3in mortar crew of 5th Battalion The Parachute Regiment. (© *Airborne Assault Museum*)

Chapter 13

Operation Market-Garden, Arnhem 17–25 September 1944

In Operation Market-Garden I Allied Airborne Corps, which included the American 82nd and 101st Airborne Divisions and the 1st British Airborne Division, was tasked to secure the main canal and river crossings between Eindhoven, Nijmegen and Arnhem in Holland. The aim was to provide an 'airborne carpet' along which the ground forces spearheaded by XXX Corps would break into the Ruhr and thus end the war.

The 1st British Airborne Division, which included the 1st, 2nd, 3rd, 10th, 11th and 156th Battalions of The Parachute Regiment under the command of Major General R E Urquhart was dropped near Arnhem to seize the road bridge over the Neder Rijn.

Due to insufficient aircraft to fly the division in one lift, the Air-Landing Brigade had to be used to protect the drop zones and landing zones for the second lift, leaving only the three battalions of the 1st Parachute Brigade to secure the bridge.

Despite the initial surprise the lightly-equipped parachutists were soon encountering unexpectedly heavy German resistance, because elements of the

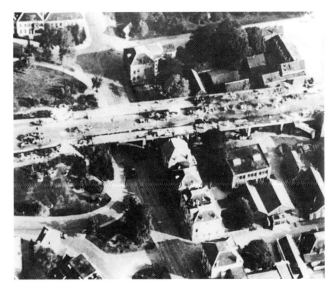

Ambushed vehicles on Arnhem road bridge. (© *Airborne Assault Museum*)

II SS Panzer Corps happened to be refitting in and around the Arnhem area. Only the 2nd Parachute Battalion commanded by Lieutenant Colonel J.D. Frost and elements of the Royal Engineers squadron, 'C' Company 3rd Parachute Battalion and other attachments reached the bridge and secured the northern end. They were soon cut off. Though under constant attack by armour and infantry the Arnhem bridge was held for three days and four nights. The division's task had been to hold for 48 hours until relieved by ground forces.

Meanwhile the rest of the division, depleted by its attempts to fight through to reinforce at the bridge, were compressed into a small perimeter across the river at Oosterbeek. They held out against overwhelming odds for nine days until ordered to withdraw across the river during the night of 25/26 September.

Of the 10,095 all ranks that landed, fewer than 3,000 got out across the river. The ground forces failed to link up and the bid to end the war in 1944 failed. Five Victoria Crosses were won during the battle, two by members of The Parachute Regiment.

Full Equipment used by Members of the 2nd Parachute Battalion, including Parachute Equipment

First pattern Denison smock, Sten bandolier, prismatic compass and pouch, toggle rope, binoculars, scrim scarf, HSAT, 37 Pattern late war fighting order, parachutist smock, Sten Mk V, 50-round .303 bandoliers, rifle valise, .303 Lee-Enfield Mk 4, beret, 2nd Battalion Battledress Blouse, Angola wool shirt, parachutist trousers, gaiters, woollen socks, ammo boots, parachutist life vest, leg bag and X Type parachute. (Note: either the rifle or the Sten gun would have been carried.) (*Author's collection*)

Offering a "smoke" to capture German female. (© *Airborne Assault Museum*)

A fantastic rare colour photograph of a fully-loaded Dakota prior to the drop into Arnhem. (Ex Mush). (*Author's collection*)

2nd Battalion Austerity Battledress Blouse and Parachutist Battledress Trousers

(Author's collection)

Sergeant, 10th Battalion The Parachute Regiment, 4th Parachute Brigade, 1st Airborne Division

Small pack (with groundsheet and gas cape attached), Sten Mk V, 37 Pattern webbing (toggle rope attached), first pattern Denison smock, scrim scarf, Gammon bomb, Hawkins mine, cigarette ration, boiled sweets ration, smaller issue cigarette tin, and Parachute Regiment beret. (*Author's collection*)

A mixed group clearing through rubble.

Map check Glider pilots on top Willys jeep. (© *Airborne Assault Museum*)

Bren Gun and valise for parachute drop. (© *Airborne Assault Museum*)

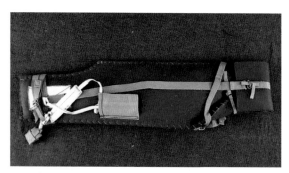

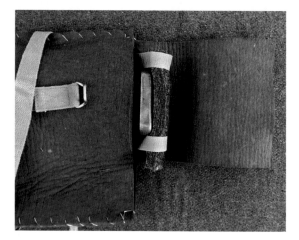

(*Author's collection*)

Members of the 1st Parachute Battalion aboard their Dakota prior to the Arnhem drop. (© *Airborne Assault Museum*)

Another photograph of members of the 1st Parachute Battalion aboard their Dakota prior to the Arnhem drop. (© *Airborne Assault Museum*)

Late War Fighting Equipment

Sten seven-pocket bandolier, 37 Pattern webbing, HSAT, small pack with gas cape, binos, map case, Sten Mk V. (*Author's collection*)

Members of the 2nd Parachute Battalion on the DZ.

Captured men at Arnhem bridge. (© *Airborne Assault Museum*)

Parachutist Jacket (Over smock)

 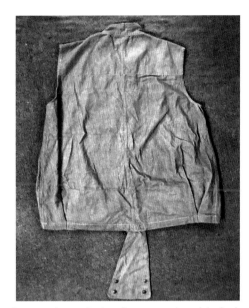

Parachutist smock worn over equipment to stop the parachute rigging lines snagging. (*Author's collection*)

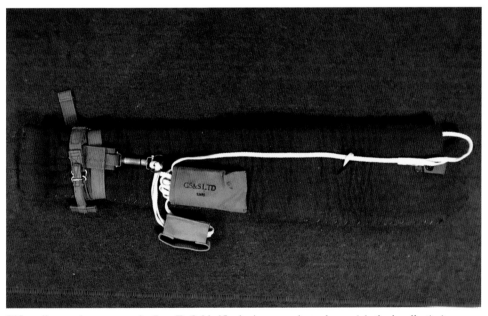

Rifle valise used to protect the Lee-Enfield rifle during parachute drops. (*Author's collection*)

Late War Leg Bag

Leg bag used by the parachutist to drop with specialist equipment or extra loads. (*Author's collection*)

Preparing for the drop. Stirling bombers in the background converted to parachutist/supply aircraft. (© *Airborne Assault Museum*)

Leg bag dated 1944 made by BR&G Ltd. (*Author's collection*)

A group of paratroopers from the 1st Parachute Battalion dug in. (© *Airborne Assault Museum*)

Rifleman Border Regiment Air landing Brigade

303 ammunition bandoliers, Mk4 Lee Enfield rifle, 37 pattern webbing (note: bayonet carried on shoulder strap and small pack fitted to lower straps, toggle rope, Helmet airborne troops, Denison smock, scrim scarf, string vest, Maroon beret Border insignia, battledress blouse with border insignia, collarless shirt, socks, Anklets, Battledress trousers, braces, underwear and ammunition boots. (*Author's collection*)

Late War Small Pack Contents

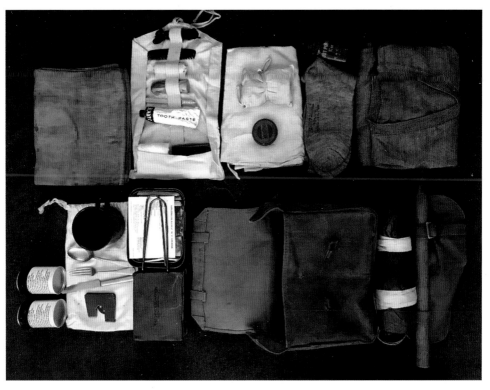

Groundsheet, 24-hour ration, fuel, folding cooker, ration bag, KFS. mess tins with another 24-hour ration, small pack, gas cape, woollen socks, towel, jumper, foot powder, housewife, personal items and wash kit. (*Author's collection*)

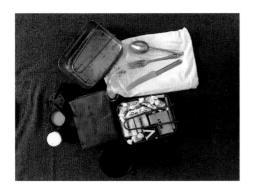 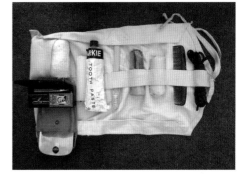

A mixed group of Para engineers and paratroopers from 'C' Company 3rd Parachute Battalion at Arnhem Bridge. (© *Airborne Assault Museum*)

Captured men of the 1st Airborne Division being searched in Arnhem. (© *Airborne Assault Museum*)

Captured engineers at the Arnhem Bridge at the end of the battle. (Note: Paratrooper in foreground wearing fibre-rimmed HSAT.) (© *Airborne Assault Museum*)

A 'stick' of Polish paratroopers boarding their Dakota prior to their delayed drop at Arnhem. (© *Airborne Assault Museum*)

Air Landing Battalions

Both the 1st and 6th Airborne Divisions had an Air Landing Brigade, made up of three line infantry battalions converted to the airborne role, specially trained and deployed by glider.

1st Airborne Division contained the 1st Air Landing Brigade made up of 1st Battalion The Border Regiment, 2nd Battalion The South Staffordshire Regiment and 7th Battalion The King's Own Scottish Borderers.

The 6th Airborne Division contained the 6th Air Landing Brigade made up of the 1st Battalion The Royal Ulster Rifles, 2nd Battalion The Oxfordshire and Buckinghamshire Light Infantry and 12th Battalion The Devonshire Regiment.

Private, 2nd Battalion South Staffords, 'B' Company, Arnhem

Assorted grenades, lightweight gas mask, 37 Pattern webbing fully packed, Celanese signal scarf, .303 ammunition bandoliers, airborne helmet, scrim scarf, first pattern Denison smock, beret, South Staffords' cap badge, battledress blouse, 'B' Company South Staffordshire insignia, collarless shirt, string vest, ammo boots, woollen socks and anklets. (*Author's collection*)

Insignia 1st Airborne Division, 2nd Independent Parachute Brigade, 6th Airborne Division

Top left down. 1st Airborne Division
1st Parachute Brigade: 1st Parachute Battalion; 2nd Parachute Battalion; 3rd Parachute Battalion.
4th Parachute Brigade: 156th Parachute Battalion; 10th Parachute Battalion; 11th Parachute Battalion.
1st Air Landing Brigade: 2nd Battalion, South Staffords Regiment; 1st Battalion, Border Regiment; 7th (Galloway) Battalion, Kings Own Scottish Borderers.
2nd Independent Parachute Brigade.
4th Parachute Battalion; 5th (Scottish) Parachute Battalion; 6th (Royal Welch) Parachute Battalion.

Top right down. 6th Airborne Division
3rd Parachute Brigade: 8th (Midlands) Parachute Battalion; 9th (Eastern Home Counties) Parachute Battalion, 1st Canadian Parachute Battalion.
5th Parachute Brigade: 12th (Yorkshire) Parachute Battalion; 13th (Lancashire) Parachute Battalion; 7th (Light Infantry) Parachute Battalion.
6th Air Landing Brigade:12th Battalion, Devonshire Regiment; 1st Battalion, Royal Ulster Rifles; 2nd Battalion, Oxfordshire and Buckinghamshire Light Infantry.
(Glider Pilot Regiment, Reconnaissance Squadron, Pathfinders. Note other support units not shown).
(*Author's collection*)

Polish Independent Parachute Brigade

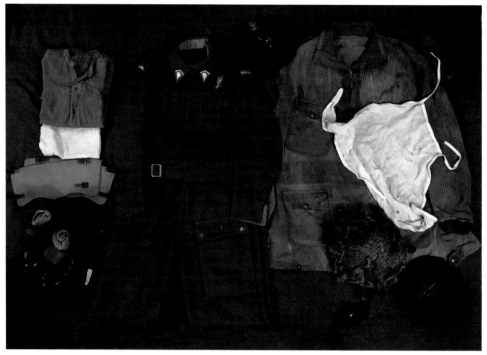

Angola wool shirt, gaiters, ammo boots, Fairbairn–Sykes knife, battledress blouse, parachutist trousers, beret, first pattern Denison smock, Celanese signal scarf, HSAT, scrim scarf and second model beret. (*Author's collection*)

Group of Polish paratroopers. (*Unknown*)

Major General Sosabowski, commander of the Polish 1st Independent Parachute Brigade, inspecting his men.

Polish paratroopers on the southern side of the lower Rhine near Arnhem. (*Unknown*)

British serge battledress blouse with Polish airborne insignia and British beret with Polish cap badge. (*Author's collection*)

Polish paratroopers aboard a Dakota. (*Unknown*)

An excellent photograph showing a Polish paratrooper's insignia. (*Unknown*)

Chapter 14

Operation Manna, Greece 1944

Operation Manna required the British 2nd Independent Parachute Brigade to drop into Greece on 12 October 1944 to assist British 23rd Armoured Brigade to stabilise the country after the German withdrawal. One company of the 4th Parachute Battalion was dropped in high winds at Megara airfield 40 miles (64km) from Athens, suffering numerous casualties. The remainder of the brigade group under Brigadier C.H.V. Pritchard followed up having been ordered to secure Athens, maintain law and order and provide necessary relief to the Greek people.

The 4th Parachute Battalion incurred some casualties in the harrying of the German forces retreating through Lamio, Larissa and Kosani. The 6th Parachute Battalion was engaged on internal security duties in Athens and Attica and the 5th Parachute Battalion arrived at Salonika in November 1944.

Vicious riots and battles broke out between rival Greek factions and communists in Athens. The brigade concentrated as a civil war developed and became involved in intense street fighting in Athens against the Greek rebels, in December and early January. The 5th Parachute Battalion suffered over 100 casualties and the 6th Parachute Battalion lost all its company commanders in fierce fighting that was widely misunderstood by the press and public opinion back home.

The mission was successfully completed by January 1945. The irony of the deployment was encapsulated by the final day's fighting in Athens when the brigade had killed 170 rebels, wounded 70 and captured 520 while concurrently feeding 20,000 civilians each day.

Paratroopers landing
in Greece. (© *Airborne
Assault Museum*)

A wounded paratrooper being given a smoke on the DZ. (© *Airborne Assault Museum*)

Paratroopers on the DZ. (© *Airborne Assault Museum*)

A paratrooper in Athens. (© *Airborne Assault Museum*)

Map check on the streets of Athens. (© *Airborne Assault Museum*)

A great group photograph of 6th Parachute Battalion on the streets of Athens. (Note: Thompson sub-machine guns). (© *Airborne Assault Museum*)

Helmet Steel Airborne Troops Late War Canvas Chinstrap

Last version of the HSAT retained the steel band but now adopted a three-point attachment webbing chinstrap. (*Author's collection*)

Paratroopers of the 6th Parachute Battalion, Athens. (© *Airborne Assault Museum*)

Megara airfield DZ. (© *Airborne Assault Museum*)

Chapter 15

The Battle of Bure, January 1945

The Battle of Bure was part of the Battle of the Bulge, which lasted from 3 to 5 January 1945 during the final months of the Second World War. The battle was fought as part of the Allied counter-attack to retake the German-held ground of the 'Bulge' which forced them on the defensive. British XXX Corps with the 6th Airborne Division attached was tasked with clearing the area east of Dinant, Rochfort, Gupont and Bure. In a tough battle Bure was secured after nearly three days of heavy fighting whilst Gupont and Rochefort were both cleared with little resistance and the advance continued.

Private, 8th Battalion The Parachute Regiment, 3rd Parachute Brigade, 6th Airborne Division

Greatcoat, HSAT, fighting order, scrim scarf, first pattern Denison smock, beret, battledress blouse, Angola wool shirt, woollen underwear, parachutist trousers, ammo boots, woollen socks and gaiters. (*Author's collection*)

Sniper of the 6th Airborne Division. (Note: issued camouflage whites.) (© *Airborne Assault Museum*)

Two from a series of photographs taken of a patrol from the 6th Airborne Division. (© *Airborne Assault Museum*)

Issue String Vest, Woollen Undershirt, Woollen Leggings and Woollen Underwear

 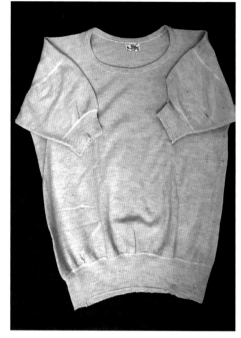

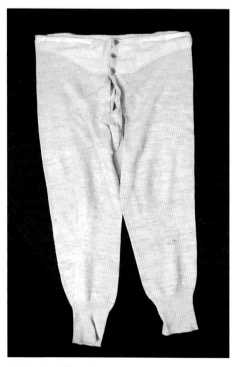 

(*Author's collection*)

Captured Germans at Bure. (© *Airborne Assault Museum*)

"Montgomery", with senior officers from the 6th Airborne Division. (© *Airborne Assault Museum*)

Sten Mk V and Bandolier

Stampings on the Sten Mk V and the seven-magazine bandolier. (*Author's collection*)

Sten loading tool, for quickly filling or emptying magazines. (*Author's collection*)

Chapter 16

Operation Varsity: The Crossing of the Rhine, 24 March 1945

O peration Varsity was a successful Allied airborne forces operation that took place towards the end of the war. Involving more than 16,000 paratroopers and several thousand aircraft, it was the largest airborne operation in history to be conducted on a single day and in one location.

Operation Varsity was part of Operation Plunder, the Anglo–American–Canadian assault under Field Marshal Bernard Montgomery to cross the Rhine and from there enter northern Germany. Varsity was meant to help the river assault troops secure a foothold across the river in western Germany by landing two airborne divisions on the eastern bank of the Rhine near the village of Hamminkeln and the town of Wesel.

The plans called for the daylight dropping of two divisions from US XVIII Airborne Corps, under Major General Matthew B. Ridgway to capture key territory and to generally disrupt German defences to aid the advance of Allied ground forces. The British 6th Airborne Division was ordered to capture the villages of Schnappenberg and Hamminkeln, clear part of the Diersfordter Wald (Diersfordt

M22 Locust airborne light tank moving in front of a Horsa glider, Operation Varsity. (© *Airborne Assault Museum*)

Forest) of German forces, and secure three bridges over the River Issel. The US 17th Airborne Division was to capture the village of Diersfordt and clear the rest of the Diersfordter Wald of any remaining German forces. The two divisions would hold the territory they had captured until relieved by advancing units of 21st Army Group, and then join in the general advance into northern Germany.

The airborne forces made several mistakes, most notably when pilot error caused paratroopers from the 513th Parachute Infantry Regiment, from the US 17th Airborne Division, to miss their drop zone and land on a British drop zone instead. However, the operation was a success, with both divisions capturing the Rhine bridges and securing towns that could have been used by the Germans to delay the advance of the British ground forces. The two divisions incurred more than 2,000 casualties but took about 3,500 prisoners. The operation was the last large-scale Allied airborne operation of the Second World War.

Pre-drop photograph of paratroopers.
(© *Airborne Assault Museum*)

Drop zone. (© *Airborne Assault Museum*)

Men of the 6th Airborne Division move through the now-captured town of Hamminkeln. (© *Airborne Assault Museum*)

Private, 7th Battalion The Parachute Regiment, 5th Parachute Brigade, 6th Airborne Division

37 Pattern webbing, HSAT, scrim scarf, second model Denison smock, Bren gun, 7th Battalion blouse, Angola wool shirt, underwear, Fairbairn-Sykes knife, ammunition boots, woollen socks and gaiters. (*Author's collection*)

A two-man gun group with Bren gun and behind them a man armed with a Projector Infantry Anti-Tank (PIAT). (© *Airborne Assault Museum*)

Parachute descent being carried out just short of the glider landing zone. (© *Airborne Assault Museum*)

'On route'. Paratrooper aboard a Dakota (Note: Sten Mk V placed under his parachute harness.) (© *Airborne Assault Museum*)

Sniper of 6th Airborne Division, Operation Varsity. (© *Airborne Assault Museum*)

Canadian second model Denison smock. (Note: Canadian Parachutist wings and the yellow epaulette tabs). (*Author's collection*)

Canadian battledress blouse. (*Author's collection*)

Canadian battledress trousers. (*Author's collection*)

Chapter 17

Advance to the Baltic, 1945

The 6th Airborne Division's objective was Wismar on the Baltic Sea. The two parachute brigades advanced on separate routes to Gadebusch, aware that the brigade to arrive first would continue as the division's lead formation. They advanced past Osnabrück, Minden and Celle and crossed the Elbe. The airborne soldiers were well suited to exploit the fluid situation that occurred following the collapse of the Rhine defences. Short fierce actions were fought from the tanks of the 4th Tank Battalion of the Grenadier Guards and whatever transport could be purloined.

A group of paratroopers take time to sample some local produce. (© *Airborne Assault Museum*)

By this stage of the war the advance was hampered more by refugees fleeing westwards than by any organised opposition. The 3rd Parachute Brigade won the race and led the division to Wismar, arriving on 1 May only 30 minutes before the lead troops of the Soviet Red Army advancing from the east. Many soldiers had completed the 350 miles (563km) on foot. The Russians were deterred from entering Lübeck. On t8 May 1945 the war in Europe ended.

While the rest of the 3rd Parachute Brigade remained at Wismar, 'B' Company of the 13th Parachute Battalion were sent to Denmark to liberate Copenhagen, arriving on 5 May. They remained in Copenhagen until the 1st Parachute Brigade arrived from England to relieve them.

Three days before the 1st Parachute Brigade, 1st Airborne Division landed at Copenhagen in Denmark to preserve law and order after outbreaks of fighting between Danish civilians and German troops. The last German garrison in Denmark surrendered on 16 May 1945.

Members of the 6th Airborne Division and Soviet troops after linking up. (© *Airborne Assault Museum*)

Advance to the Baltic. (© *Airborne Assault Museum*)

US-issued Flashlight and Late War British Issue Torch

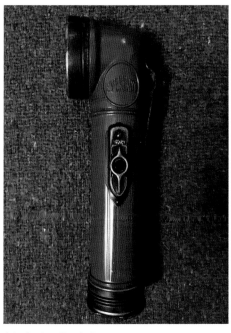 

(*Author's collection*)

British pathfinders carrying US flashlights. (© *Airborne Assault Museum*)

Field Marshal Montgomery visiting members of the 6th Airborne Division. (© *Airborne Assault Museum*)

A couple of paratroopers surrounded by surrendered German troops and a possible Para dog. (© *Airborne Assault Museum*)

Lightweight Service Respirator

(*Author's collection*)

Haversack, late war anti-gas brassards, anti-gas eye shields, haversack, anti-dimming cloth in tin, lightweight service respirator, anti-gas ointment, and cotton waste. (*Author's collection*)

Chapter 18

Operation Doomsday, Norway 1945

Major General Urquhart received his orders to deploy to Norway in the midst of a division reorganization. The 1st Parachute Brigade had been despatched to Denmark on 5 May 1945, 1st Polish Brigade was alerted for an overseas move and the Special Air Service Brigade, then in Germany, was attached to the division to compensate. Despite the chaos attendant with the fluid situation of the German defeat, 1st Airborne Division prepared and launched the Norwegian mission within four days of receiving the Warning Order.

Advance parties flew into Norway on 9th May but the division's follow-up was delayed by inclement weather. The task was to maintain law and order, secure airfields, prevent sabotage and oversee the German surrender. This was potentially a dangerous assignment as 6,000 airborne troops were being called upon to disarm and control 350,000 German soldiers. The division assisted in the recovery of prisoners of war, apprehended war criminals, allocated German units to staging reservations and employed them to clear their own minefields.

Air accidents occurred resulting in the deaths of one officer and thirty-three men, and the AOC 38 Group RAF was killed with six others killed and seven missing.

1st Airborne Division retained control until the arrival of HQ Allied Land Forces in Norway as well as conducting the welcoming ceremony for the return of the King of Norway from exile.

Paratroopers of the 1st Airborne Division after landing in Norway. (*Unknown*)

Munitions and Ration and Pocket Items

No. 82 Gammon bomb, Hawkins mine, Mills grenades, blast grenade and No. 77 phosphorous grenade. (*Author's collection*)

Various issue ration items carried on the paratrooper's person. (*Author's collection*)

Early issue water–purifying tablets carried in the Denison smock pocket. (*Author's collection*)

Issued boiled sweets ration tin used to carry cigarettes, lighter and Morphine within its own tin and usual personal documents carried within the battledress blouse pocket: paybook, first aid memoire and service envelopes. (*Author's collection*)

Chapter 19

Sangshak, 1944

The Battle of Sangshak was fought in the mountainous area between India and Burma from 20 to 26 March 1944. Japanese forces engaged the British Indian Army forcing the Parachute Brigade out of its positions and suffering huge casualties as a result. This battle imposed a delay on the Japanese forces, allowing the British and India forces to reinforce a vital position at Kohima.

Unknown to Japanese intelligence, battalions of 50th Indian Brigade were exercising and patrolling with light equipment around Kohima. The Japanese 15th and 31st Divisions found them in their path while conducting an east-west infiltration attack across the jungle-covered Naga Hills beyond the River Chindwin, heading towards India.

'C' Company 152nd Parachute Battalion was overrun on a high plateau near Ukhrul. Only 20 men survived but they killed 450 Japanese.

The Brigade was hastily ordered to concentrate whilst still under fire at the key point of the village of Sangshak, perched on a steep hillside between Imphal and the Chindwin. They were ordered to hold the Japanese onslaught at all costs.

The Indian Parachute Brigade group held up the Japanese advance for six days, in appalling conditions, inflicting heavy casualties on the enemy but at great loss. Fierce hand-to-hand fighting revolved around the Sangshak church with 200 yards of brigade headquarters. Counter-attacks with bayonet and kukri drove the Japanese back.

Air supply drops fell wide, casualties could not be evacuated and reinforcements failed to get through. The brigade held on doggedly as ammunition, food and water ran out.

On 26 March, with both sides nearing complete exhaustion, the arrival of the 5th Indian Division in Imphal fulfilled the Brigade's delaying mission. That night it was ordered to 'fight its way out' back to Imphal, having lost 40 officers and 585 men.

The Japanese thrust at Imphal was blunted by this action that cost them 2,000 men, notably leaders. The 50th Indian Parachute Brigade's achievement was recognized in a Special Order of the Day issued by Field Marshal Sir William Slim on 31 August.

The Japanese offensive was defeated at Imphal and Kohima. Survivors from the brigade took part in the final stage of the Burma campaign, successfully parachuting into Rangoon.

Officer inspecting parachute harnesses of waiting Gurkha parachutists. (© *Airborne Assault Museum*)

RAF sergeant inspecting British Indian parachutist harnesses. (© *Airborne Assault Museum*)

A 'stick' of Gurkha parachutists waiting to board their aircraft. (© *Airborne Assault Museum*)

Gurkha parachutist in front of a Dakota. (© *Airborne Assault Museum*)

Gurkha parachutists aboard their aircraft. (© *Airborne Assault Museum*)

Gurkhas pre-
drop.

Pre-flight checks

Chapter 20

The Far East, 1945

The 5th Parachute Brigade was sent to the Far East, arriving after VJ Day. They were to protect and secure Dutch East Indies interests and property, as well as dealing with internal security in Java and Singapore, whilst disarming Japanese troops until 1946. Then they were sent back to Palestine to take part in peacekeeping with the rest of the 6th Airborne Division.

They were involved in clearing up the Japanese in Northern Malaya and on internal security duties in Singapore until December 1945. They were then despatched to restore law and order and civil government in Semerang in North Java, now torn by civil strife and rival political extremist factions. This task was completed by May 1946 and subsequently the brigade returned to the UK and was disbanded; its 7th Battalion replacing the 17th (in 1st Brigade). The 17th together with the 12th and 13th Battalions then ceased to exist in the Regular Army.

Checkpoint manned by paratroopers of the 5th Parachute Brigade. (© *Airborne Assault Museum*)

Jungle aertex shirt, 44 jungle trousers, scrim scarf, 44 Pattern webbing, ammo boots, gaiters, beret, jungle hat, 44 Pattern small pack (poncho/blanket attached) and Sten Mk V. (*Author's collection*)

Clearance patrol lead by officer armed with Browning pistol. (© *Airborne Assault Museum*)

44 Pattern Webbing

44 Pattern small
pack with toggle
rope attached. Note
44 Pattern rubber
poncho attached
below. 44 Pattern
webbing consisting of
ammunition pouch,
compass pouch,
water bottle pouches,
machete, ammunition
pouch and a Sten
Mk V. (*Author's
collection*)

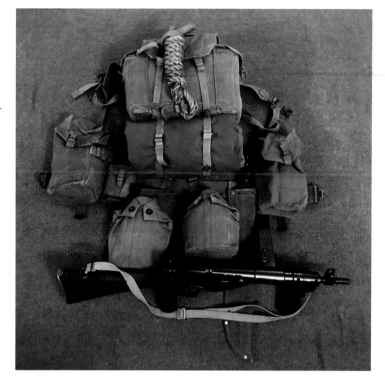

(© *Airborne Assault Museum*)

44 Pattern Water Bottle Items

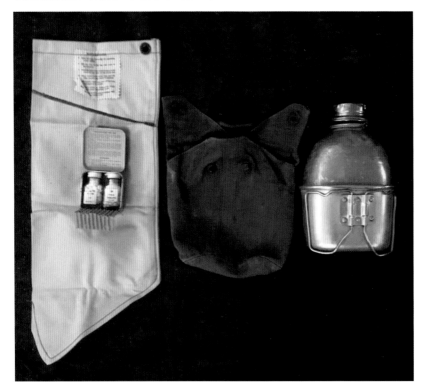

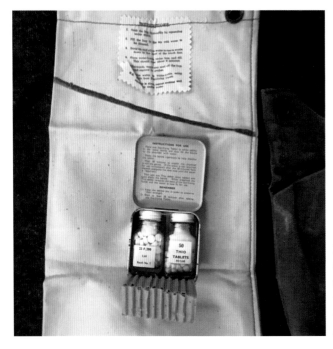

Millbank bag for filtering water, and purification tablets both carried in a small pocket in the water bottle pouch. 44 Pattern water bottle and mug. (*Author's collection*)

5th Parachute Brigade members fully loaded. (© *Airborne Assault Museum*)

Members of the 5th Parachute Brigade landing by sea. (© *Airborne Assault Museum*)

Men of 5th Parachute Brigade route march in full marching order. (© *Airborne Assault Museum*)

Clearance patrol cautiously checking through a hamlet for any Japanese hostiles. (© *Airborne Assault Museum*)